London Laureate Laurie Bolger was
currently hosts BANG Said the Gu
poetry night and multi-award-winr
@ *Laurie's* live from Camden's Roundhouse. Laurie was recently
appointed lead facilitator for BBC 1Xtra's Words First London.

www.lauriebolger.com

Box Rooms

Laurie Bolger

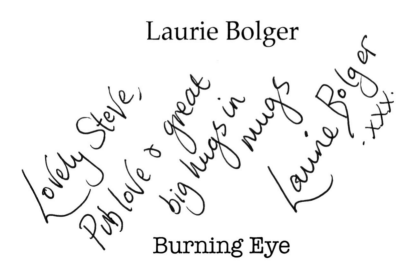

Lovely Steve,
Pub love & great
big hugs in mugs
Laurie Bolger xxx.

Burning Eye

This edition published by Burning Eye Books 2016

www.burningeye.co.uk
@burningeyebooks

Burning Eye Books
15 West Hill, Portishead, BS20 6LG

ISBN 978-1-909136-78-6

For Rich

Contents

Trees

Somebody told me once that perfect love
is two trees growing side by side
in their own time, never leaning on the other one.

I think that sounds bloody lovely,
but it doesn't actually happen like that.

If you ask me, love is wasps and grasshoppers.
It's anger, patience and stings and finding the legs
to jump into things and get stuff done.

Today is another duvet day, we read stale news
and stay indoors. We talk less now, cuddle more,
remember when our legs did all sorts.

Outside our cluttered bedroom, the council
are chopping at the London planes,
they have to hack them back to make more space.

As they drop one by one onto the pavement,
I think, *pretty soon we will be light and air again.*

Embers

after Tom Weir

The turf fire burns out
and holds the last heat
like whisky dregs –

it's not ready to go out yet,
there's still a little bit of warmth left –
so we gather round to savour

the last spark. I remember
when we fed that fire
until it was fierce

with everything we could find,
we loved to watch the crisp packets
set alight inside

and then die
like our little laughs
when she told us not to do that.

Sometimes we thought its flames
would set fire to the ceiling lamp
or the piles of cards that we hid in our laps.

Now, grown up,
we are having a nightcap,
we know it won't be long,
but we don't say anything like that –

we just speak by her bed
in hushed heavy breaths,
the small crackle of firewood
inside her bony chest –

W10

Those thick-skinned women who brought out
suds and sponges in buckets, rested them in doorways,

kneeling in their slippers, they'd scrub and scrub.
It was all about keeping the modest porch dirt-free daily

and looking well. The old dears of W10, so much pride.
The ones who told tales of real life in their kitchens,

carried generosity in their bellies and plates of
buffet food two by two.

The Posh End

Totally alone, you stitch and hem the pretty rear garden
in view of neighbours who irritate the shit out of you.
You scrub at the patio, iron tea towels, write lists.

Your new bedside table props up that exhausted copy
of *Cathy Come Home* and I know you still keep a key
for the old back gate, I found it. The one you and Dad
saved for, it took you months.

Sometimes I hear you rummaging through the night.
You hate him for snoring and you never forgave him
for pulling you away from the noise.

Stapleton Road

I'm leaning on the wall
of your mishmash concrete garden,
watching you puff and pace
and potter with the plants.
Your face is scrunched up in the sun,
you are frayed around the edges.
I'll have to get my train soon.

The piles of mugs in your kitchen
all have their handles missing,
so you drain your tea –
half look at me – picking
at the buddleia by the wall,
stubborn little thing, familiar
with the city, pushing its way
through the concrete.

I know I'll walk the platform tonight
and read your station on my ticket,
the cement at Waterloo will tell me
to forget you. I'll throw my coffee cup
in the bin and then try to press
that same unsteady feeling I get
every time that I pull in.

Wheelie Bins

You are parachute eyes and fingertips
and let's not talk about this now.

We are ten green bottles sitting on a wall,
let's drink down all the booze in Bristol,
we met at a festival after all.

In your museum bedroom
I try to fasten us together,
just to see if we could hold
past twenty-four hours.

We are the ice tray not quite set,
we are awkward morning conversations
and heavy bags on doorsteps, we are
queuing at the bar. Tonight it's

flutters of temper over nightcaps, us two
rosy rag dolls who would rather do this
than be on their own.

Do you remember falling light
and letting go?
Do you remember grass and potions
and rabbit holes?
Rounds of messy roulette,
losing it all to the dance tent.

I could get that bloody Megabus home,
or I could make us float,
or just throw my shoes across the room at you
like they do in soaps.

Rubbish

And so live ever — or else swoon to death,
that's what he said, Keats.

Although I bet he never tripped
over the recycling on his way in
and tonight, Cilla, I'm full-on plummeting
through the concrete.

The stars are so much brighter where you live,
they're giving everything they've got

but you are complaining about money, and that taxi
that took us all round the houses for the sake of it.

Tonight we took down every single shot and swig,
sang rubbish lyrics to sweaty ceilings
in dance floor crowds we couldn't breathe in.

Then we ditched trays of cheesy chips
like pennies lobbed into a fountain,
a sixpence buried in the Christmas pudding.

I made a wish.

We Watched a Wasp in the Bedroom Lamp

Stared at it, while you held that chipped cup
slopped full of green organic soup,
you'd been stirring it for ages now.

You sat up in bed, my hand close
to your head, I played with your hair
and we made bad jokes.

The high-pitched tie-dye woman from next door
brought round a spray of pale yellow and lilac,
a bouquet from a farmers' market.

Mine were wrapped in cellophane,
a sachet of flower food stuck round the bottom.
'There's some proper flowers,' she said
and plonked hers down on the windowsill.

You gave me a dazed happy smile, as if you knew.

Body heat and the smell of your shampoo
filled your sun-raked room, with a wasp
in a bedside light and two sets of flowers in the window.

Booze and You

Your face is a scribble when you sleep.
I'm watching the bare bulb on your flaky ceiling
and you're snoring, sucking the paint off the walls.

This morning we're unstuck, washed up damp like driftwood,
and sticking-wise I don't think that we could.

Along to the radiator's hum and click,
I'm anchored to your bedspread waiting
for the hangover to hit. Last night's ashtray

filled up with your funny moods and my lipstick.
The blind's gone to shit, looks like it could come
crashing down on us any minute. It's way past fixing

but so are we so we keep on gathering ourselves in sheets,
the creases round your eyelids are lifelines
to me. Especially when life's been a bit of a scrapheap.

Pass the flower and pull the petal, the finest ones
always make us go mental in the end. *He loves me, he loves me not,*
   he loves me, he loves me not, he loves me, he loves me not, diamond
   ring, vodka shot.

Neither of us are making tea.

No one's gone out jogging in a vest down the artisan bakery
for bags of poncey pastries. There's no soft white curtain
floating in the breeze, singing to itself.

It's not like the films, is it?

There's no sea view
        just me   and you
in a box room, bed unmade and locked in,
with a message in a bottle asking you to pull me in.

The Old Man

You listen to deaths announced on the kitchen radio,
you know most of them, tell me that's what you get
for being old. The tap of your soft soles on the lino,
you've had that pair for ages, the only shoes I think
I've ever seen you in – scuffed black and bent up.

You tell me how you walked to the schoolhouse all
those years ago – you and your brothers, barefoot,
not one pair between the lot of you.

You in your jacket and cap, ragged old stick in hand –
we walk the lanes. I mean to ask you a hundred
thousand questions before you go for good, just so
I can say that I did, just so I can say I knew everything.

I run ahead pretending I'm Mary Lennox, kicking the
heads off dandelions and dancing round your legs.
The ditches either side make the lane into a maze,
not a gap in the green.

When I've gone too far I leg it back to you. You puff tiny
clouds my way, pup-pupping that worn-out old pipe,
and when you're not looking I take off my shoes,
just to see what it's like.

This Morning Your Mum Gave Me
Your Hairbrush

In the shower I shut my eyes,
hoping to run into a wall of stars
instead of the dark drift of funeral cars,

and your hippy brand of shampoo
took me straight to you, so I stayed
under the water for ages.

The plughole pulled at suds
that mapped the floor, and hair,
some mine and some yours.

Then stood in a towel by your bed,
I held its teeth close to my head.

Today will never be long enough
but they told me it takes time,
so slowly I brushed your roots in mine.

For Jess

We drank whisky by the oven the night you went,
my arm around your mum, holding her steady
with the shock of it.

Since then, mate, it's hit us like a bloody tube train.
One under, constant rush hour. We've all moved back
to this tourist town and are working silly hours.

I'm living with your auntie just while I'm looking –
the one whose cupboards are full of antique air
and spices. I'm pretty sure most have been there
since the eighties.

The freezer is packed iceberg-style
from that springtime you lived there,
she won't clean it out.

She found some old spinach
lodged at the back of the drawer
and told me she couldn't bin it.

This moth has started nibbling at my best jacket,
in the wardrobe attic bedroom I dread coming home to
just in case she gets the photo albums out again,

shows me your thirty-one years in pictures
then asks me loads of questions –
before another long conversation about the NHS.

She plays a lot of classical music,
which between you and me is doing my head in,
so I potter around the kitchen and smoke out the back,
careful not to tread on the snails who paint the patio at night.

And the time she had to call the locksmith
because in trying to be quiet, hammered drunk,
I put my door key in the lock and it snapped.
(She did too. She went mad.)

I'd love to call you for a chat.

I've been dreaming of you for weeks,
of corridors and flashes of blue and all the little things
I'd say to you if I could.

Tea

He's watching that Bill Bailey DVD again,
but we all watch comedy in a crisis, don't we?

Try to turn our minds off or take comfort
in making the other one five hundred cups of tea,
spending whole days in our trackies.

I tell him, 'Look, mate, you'll feel much better
if you quickly jump in the shower, seriously.'
(I've not even brushed my teeth.)

I want someone to plop me into a full teacup,
stir it up and dissolve me in
and in the most delightful way.

I will hold your hand, mate.

We've had so many flowers we've run out of vases.
I reach for the household teapot, sprinkle some stones
into the bottom to help hold the stems up.

I want someone to tell me a story,
because there's a photo of her
in the middle of the buffet table
but nobody knows where to start.

So we whisper in small talk, play the part,
lean awkwardly through lack of chairs
and talk about how the weather's held out
(whatever that means).

Carrot Mash

These days we board tube trains with brave faces,
make phone calls to each other on lunch breaks.

I tell you I'm gonna cook us a nice meal tonight,
a rescue remedy stew scenario, some sort of stodge.

I'll cook the veg until soft, then I'll add salt, pepper,
a big dollop of butter, thank you Jamie Oliver. Done.

I ask a bloke with gelled ginger hair and orange fleece,
he's reducing bags of broccoli by the fridge.

'Excuse me, can you help me? I'm looking for carrots.'
He tells me they haven't got any.

It's when he suggests parsnips.
'In the nicest possible way, that's not the same,' I say.

I look and see that they sell star anise –

'HOW THE HELL CAN YOU POSSIBLY HAVE STAR ANISE
    AND NO SODDING CARROTS?'

I've lost it in the veg aisle.

Toast

In the kitchen they talk about the gym
and trendy parties. To be honest with you,
I'm more bad skin and ovaries.
The Notorious PMT.

In the kitchen it's three in the morning,
there's burnt toast in the bin, I'm not sure
what I'm doing but I'm crying over him.

In the kitchen it's another application form
being thrown into oblivion, your chance to be
a TV runner is one in ten hundred billion.

'It's all about getting your foot on the ladder,' she said.
'It's just another string to your bow,' he went.

I do not want babies yet.

In the kitchen we're cohabiting, two worried snails
waiting on the dry city concrete, lost and
about to be squashed by other people's feet.

In the kitchen we are ancient trees,
tired out and pulled from their roots.
I promised I'd never make a chore out of you.

In a kitchen there's another shit party in East London.
I've got a shedload of lipstick on and they're kissing
on couches with beards ten a dozen. Those pouty girls

in jelly shoes, life's logos sprawled across tiny boobs
that don't move. They're giving it all, without giving
much away.

In the kitchen plates are spinning, plates are
smashing, she asks, 'Sorry, did you say something?'

I wish I'd brought more booze,
or even that I was sitting next to you.

The party host has bought one of those basil plants
that won't last past the last pasta dish she put it in.

It's knackered on the windowsill,
it reminds me of him.

Living in a Shoebox

I make tea in those mugs
they bought us when we moved in,
              HIS and *HERS* ones.

Our conversation is tied in familiar knots,
              sat opposite, house warming,
we stir a couple of sugars in, try our best to laugh it off.

              Do you remember our first night here?
When it was all empty rooms
              and no central heating?

We were butterflies surviving winter
              but now it's spring,
and you've come to get your stuff.

I'll ring when your post arrives,
              mate, we're so past fuss,
with all the bits and bobs
              to be moved about and boxed up.

You will come and go in this brilliant box
              that built us.

So you go into the hallway to sort through your shoes,
              that's the bit that really gets me.

I help you brush the dust
                from the pairs you didn't wear much,
try to make them new.

When you go you give me a look that fastens us,
                the invisible cords of a long time.
I tuck myself under your arm and you pull me in.

It's the familiar dance we do,
                we've been doing it for years.

Then it's just me.

So let me tell a story, the one where we worked
selling shoes, once upon a time
                we packed pairs into boxes.

I'd leg it down to the stockroom
                whenever you came in,
to apply scruffy makeup
        between the winter boots and practical pumps.

We didn't really say much,
        just the odd comment about the work rota
or what time we'd be hitting the pub.

We'd check for sizes over the phone,
                a *shoe check*, that's how we met.

By the front door intercom I'm all over the place,
now my makeup is sprawled right up my face.

I tell you to go quick
        or you'll start me off,

in this love among the ruins and bags of stuff.

Lost Property

We pick at the Sunday chicken bones left in the fridge,
try to find the wish bone and worry about

the Monday morning's commute, where we'll have to
check for our heartbeats on the tube.

When we can't find them we'll go to that big room
at Baker Street to ask the TFL man if anyone's
handed them in.

All the umbrellas will be labelled like school
and there'll be suitcases full of false teeth.

TFL man will tell us that some mornings
the phones all ring at once.

At your house I look for the bathroom light in the dark.
Take all your personal belongings with you.
                    Doors closing. Mind the gap.

Slippers

You wave me off one more brave-faced time, from the
sitting-room window
as the bashed-up hire car backs out of the driveway and
makes dents in the gravel.
You are masked by net curtains. They do you in,
goodbyes like this.

In a couple of days I'll ring you from the Avenues and
you'll ask
when I'm coming to see you next, but I've only just left.

Next time I do, your address will be New Ross
Community Hospital,
where we'll walk a long corridor. I'll listen to the pat of
your stick on the floor,
the shuffle of your slippers.

I will hold your hand. It'll be as freezing as your room,
where ever so slowly
you'll clear a space for me on the bed and offer me
boiled sweets
like you used to on the ferry.

But you won't play that trick this time, the one where
you pull away your hand when I go for the bag,

you'll have forgotten that.

Blackberries

I held you like a breath in the back of the car,
waiting for that phone call to reach us.
The cabbie put his foot down when I told him.

At home she said she saw blackberries. I'm still
not sure if she meant the small fruits yellowing down
the side of the house or her mobile handset.

'We'll be there soon,' on repeat. I wanted to convince you
that I could fix things, or even that we'd get there
before the flowers did. It seemed like five minutes ago

we were all crumbs in bed, arguing over the battered mattress,
or the telly, the gaps in the floor. Along to Heart FM
and the breath of the air con, we were still.

I wanted to say to you that what you did was enough.
The sky turned to dishwater, and quicksand filled our guts,
'He sends his love.' Did you hold on for that?

Time

I think he had all the time in the world to get drunk
with anyone who would listen,
so I told him everything,
in the end.

In the pub that band was on.
I asked the barman
to borrow a pen.

The old man next to me with whisky on his breath
came close to my face when he offered me a chair.
'I'm OK,' I told him.

He went into his jacket, pulled out a little bookie's pen,
blue plastic, and when the barman came back
with a pub-branded pencil he smiled and said,
'Whatever she's having.'

His face was the type that had been earnt
so I said, 'Go on then, you old charmer,
one won't hurt.'

The pub was falling apart,
a story for every single glass
and ever since the clock hands stopped
time had gone out the window.

Someone told me once that time was there for a reason
so that life's little dramas don't all come at once.

We exchanged the type of trust that only we can in pubs,
people like us.

We bartered our baggage until the last trains had gone,
and I went to leave the pub without his name in the end.

He told me he always sat in that same old spot,
'Come back for a chat, darling, whenever you want.'

Public House

The Princes and Dukes
have given
their last orders,
handed over
to the builders.
Their chimes
have gone
quiet.

The grated
wooden sign
wobbles outside
while they prise off
the tavern's tiles,
hacking them off
in chunks.

So here's one
for the locals.
The ones
who
smoked
down
to logos
in doorways.

Let's toast to the bar stalls
who propped up last orders
to the regular pull of the pumps.

Did you hear
the carpet cry
when they pulled
it up?
Each fibre
a sing-song stuck
and then drowned
in cement.

Here's to the door
that opens easily.
To Friday nights
dolled up
for karaoke,
and the licence
to let go.

The Tarted-Up Boozer in Shoreditch

We ditched the familiar smell
of stale beer and sodden bar towels
for a molten-orange glowing counter top
with *BAR* written in neon lights
on top of a fish-tank, home to five
of the most miserable marine creatures
I had ever seen, poor boozy bar fish
taking it all in.

We ditched the rabble and the riot
of our West End local
for a bunch of moody indie kids
with shit haircuts and boardgames
rolling cigarettes and posing
as the singer/actor/part-time model –
girls in green Barbour coats
with bird-nest hair
sipping brown ale,
they'd like a Bacardi Breezer secretly
and they burn incense sticks
so you can barely tell your pint
from sandalwood.

We ditched our plump busty landlady
who sweats under bright lights
and breathes heavy as she pulls me a pint.
We ditched her for an indie cindie barman
dressed in Grandad-style knitwear,

a dickie-bow tie
and Topshop's finest pair of thick black glasses
too big for his face.

You look a bit like Jarvis Cocker, mate,
and those are not prescription lenses
in those frames.

He's mechanic and uncharming,
looks alarmed when I ask him,
'What's your cheapest pint, mate?'

He tells me, 'We only do
bottles of beer and they're all, like,
four pounds.'

It's all very dark,
we take in
the candlelit ambience,
with a mannequin,
a moose head wearing a top hat,
and lampshades like my nan had.

The DJ is dropping beats
behind the smallest DJ booth
I've ever seen.
Next to the gents'
he's working the decks,

like he's working
the crowd at Creamfields.
Everyone is sat down.

I begin to miss the local pub's jukebox mix
of punk, funk, folk, the occasional Irish,
the locals' sing-song, soles beating
the battered carpet.

This place has the slipperiest floor
I have ever walked across
and I'm wearing high shoes
'cause it's a little bit posh here.

I slide into the loos
where girls paint pretentious stares
and flick their hair and look really,
genuinely, actually posh.

We go and do some shots
with indie boy Jarvis, who's still
one hundred percent deadpan.

He doesn't tell us his life story
like the old bloke in our local,
and I could spend a year here
trying to meet an old friend,
or create something humble,
but we leave because it's shit.

We ramble home through city drizzle,
street lights make puddles jaundice-yellow

and I can breathe again.

Paraffin-blue lights
cut through dark
and make me jump,
so I climb onto the night bus,
take my shoes off,
and travel across this tourist town,

to our grubby little local,
just around the corner,

where we know
we are guaranteed
to get a lock-in.

Tables

We are all Edward Hoppers here
painting pictures of ourselves.
'It's OK, I'm waiting for someone.'

The room is packed full
of dim-lit couples chatting away
across wobbly tables.

At the door you wipe your feet.
There's nothing I like more
than watching you
looking for me.

Bricks

London Bridge is ice tonight.
I puff warm air in tiny clouds
when I pass the dusty Underground.

I like being on my own down here,
watching the night-walkers in pairs
pointing at the boats on Father Thames –

star-dippers,
submarines,
and pirate ships.

The city lot are thick with coats,
all darting down side streets
as speeding car lights
look like gold-red beads on a necklace.

And all those grey bricks,
the box rooms balanced
on box rooms.

Do you remember
when we brought
that flat pack home
to our bare bedroom,
when it was all in bits,
and we built it?

Acknowledgements

Thanks to Clive and Burning Eye Books for making this happen. Thanks to Lis Watkins for making beautiful artwork. Thanks to Stuart Silver and Caroline Bird for all the solid advice and feedback, you've been amazing. Thanks to Roundhouse for massive support. Thanks to Daisy Dockrill for being a top bird. Thanks to Wandering Word and Bristol. Thanks to Roundhouse Radio, BBC Radio 1 and 1Xtra because poetry was made for radio. Thanks to Hollie McNish for always being lush. Thanks to the Ivy House locals and Geoff at the Bar. Thanks to Laura Kenwright #Megababe. Thanks to Jenny and the McDonaghs. Thanks to Rosalind, Colin and Tommy for making me slow down and remember what's important. Thanks to Matt Roffe for being so on it and building things. Thanks to 'Porky the Poet' Phill Jupitus. Thanks to Marcus Davey. Thanks to Jackie and Hayley in the shop. Thanks to Fran, Zia, Jacob and the housemates. Thanks to BANG Said the Gun, Young Poet Laureate, Spread the Word, the Poetry Takeaway and Apples and Snakes for being so ace.

Thanks to Mum, Dad and Gem for everything.

Thanks to Richard Gunn for being my best mate.

Lightning Source UK Ltd.
Milton Keynes UK
UKOW01f0328280616

277226UK00003B/31/P